Ladders

The U.S. Constitution
Famous Documents

MEET THE CON

by Sheri Reda

What if no one were in charge at your school or in your classroom? School would be a chaotic place with no control over what happened there. It's the same for our country. We have a government, laws, and rules to maintain order. A country couldn't survive without people in charge—a government—making sure that life is fair and society works effectively. Without a government, there would be no order, and our lives would be turned upside down.

This country's Founders knew the importance of a strong government, so more than 200 years ago they wrote the U.S. Constitution. This document established our federal government. In the part of the Constitution called the Articles, the United States is established as a **republic** in which people elect their representatives. The Constitution also created three equal branches to balance power. These branches work together to make and carry out the rules and laws. The photo and captions on the right identify these three branches—the executive, legislative, and judicial—and explain some of the powers each branch holds.

THE EXECUTIVE BRANCH

In January 2013, Barack Obama was sworn in for his second term as president in Washington, D.C. During the ceremony, President Obama took the **oath** of office, promising to preserve, protect, and defend the Constitution. As head of the executive branch, the president can sign bills into law, as well as **veto**, or reject, a bill. The president is also the commander-in-chief of the United States Armed Forces.

President Obama

∧ President Barack Obama is joined by his wife, First Lady Michelle Obama, and their two daughters as he takes the oath of office for the second time.

STITUTION

THE LEGISLATIVE BRANCH

Representative John Boehner and Senator Chuck Schumer looked on as President Obama took the oath of office. Both work in the U.S. Congress, the legislative branch, which is made up of the Senate and the House of Representatives. As detailed in the Constitution's Articles, the elected officials in these two chambers introduce, review, and pass bills before the bills come to the president to be signed into law or vetoed.

Representative Boehner

Senator Schumer

THE JUDICIAL BRANCH

Chief Justice John Roberts administered the oath of office to the president. Roberts leads the other eight judges who make up the Supreme Court, which is part of the judicial branch. The Supreme Court decides whether laws are fair and makes sure they follow the Constitution.

Chief Justice Roberts

A CLOSER LOOK

Our Constitution brings us together as a country and guarantees that all U.S. citizens enjoy the same basic rights. It has established our laws and guided our government since 1787, but it has also been changed many times to reflect changes in the ways we live. Let's take a closer look at our Constitution and all of its parts and updates.

THE PREAMBLE

"We the People" are the first words of the Constitution's preamble, or introduction, but who are "the People"? The definition has changed over time. Today all adult citizens make up "the People." They govern by electing the country's leaders. That's what makes our government a republic.

THE ARTICLES

The Constitution's seven articles, or sections, describe how our government works. The first three of these articles establish the government's three branches. These are the legislative, executive, and judicial branches.

THE AMENDMENTS

Over time, changes called **amendments** have been added to the U.S. Constitution. Here are the 27 amendments made to the Constitution so far. The first ten amendments are called the Bill of Rights. The Bill of Rights spells out basic individual rights. The original wording of all the amendments is hard to read, so we're going to look at them in more everyday language.

1. You have the right to freedom of religion, assembly, petition, the press, and speech. (1791)

2. You have the right to bear arms. (1791)

3. You cannot be forced to allow soldiers to stay in your home during peacetime. (1791)

4. You have the right to be safe from unreasonable searches and seizures, which means that police or other government officials cannot search you or your home for no reason. (1791)

5. You have the right to due process of law. That includes the right to remain silent and not testify against yourself if you are arrested. (1791)

6. If accused of a crime, you have the right to a lawyer and a speedy and fair trial. (1791)

7. You have the right to trial by jury. (1791)

8. You have the right to be safe from cruel punishment and excessive fines. (1791)

9. You have other rights besides those listed in the Constitution. (1791)

10. Powers that the Constitution does not give to the U.S. government go instead to state governments. (1791)

11. The United States has no power in lawsuits against individual states. (1795)

12. Representatives called electors meet in their states and cast two votes—one for president and one for vice-president. (1804)

13. Slavery is banned. (1865)

14. No state can take away the rights of U.S. citizens. (1868)

15. U.S. citizens cannot be denied the right to vote because of race. (1870)

16. The U.S. government can collect taxes on money people earn. (1913)

17. The people of each state elect two U.S. senators, who serve for six years. (1913)

18. It is illegal to make, sell, or transport alcoholic beverages. (1919)

19. Women have the right to vote. (1920)

20. Each elected president takes office on January 20th of the year following the election. (1933)

21. The 18th Amendment is struck down, making it legal to make, sell, and transport alcoholic drinks. (1933)

22. A president can serve only two terms in office. (1951)

23. The people of Washington, D.C., can vote in elections for president. (1961)

24. Citizens have the right to vote without paying any taxes or fees for that right. (1964)

25. If the president dies or is unable to perform the duties of office, the vice-president takes over. (1967)

26. Citizens have the right to vote at age 18 or older. (1971)

27. If members of Congress vote to raise their own pay, the raise begins after the next election. (1992)

Check In Why is the Constitution so important to our country?

Read to find out about the debates that helped shape the U.S. Constitution.

Conflict and Compromise

by Becky Manfredini · illustrated by John Jay Cabuay

> **Welcome, everyone! James Madison at your service. Since they call me the "Father of the Constitution," I'll be your guide as you listen in on the debates that helped Founders like me create that document.**

In 1787, leaders of every state except Rhode Island met in Philadelphia, Pennsylvania, to make a new plan, or constitution, for the United States. For six years, the government had been organized under the Articles of Confederation, but that plan created a weak government that did not have the power to form an army to stop rebellions. It also couldn't collect taxes. So the representatives at this Constitutional **Convention** got together to create a stronger government. Right from the beginning, a debate raged over how to form our legislature, or lawmaking body. Small states wanted a legislature with the same number of representatives from each state, so each state would have equal power. But the large states believed states with more people should also have more representatives and more power. Let's find out what happened.

The only way to give the people a voice is to base the number of representatives from a state on how many people live in that state!

That is unfair and unacceptable. Every state should have an equal number of representatives, no matter how big or small it is!

New Jersey Delegates

Virginia Delegates

Finally, the small states and the large states agreed on a **compromise**. In other words, each side agreed to give up something they wanted in order to reach an agreement. According to this compromise, we agreed to have two lawmaking bodies whose members are elected by the people. One would be the House of Representatives, based on the number of people in each state, and the other would be the Senate, with two representatives from each state. And so, with this compromise, we had some peace—for a while at least.

The next big argument was about how many representatives each state would have in the House of Representatives. We had agreed that the number of representatives would be based on the population of the states. But should enslaved people be counted as part of a state's population? Southern states wanted to count enslaved people. That way, the Southern states would get more representatives in the House of Representatives—and more power.

You don't count enslaved people as citizens, so you can't count them as part of your population!

Northern Delegates

We overcame many challenges while we worked to create the U.S. Constitution, but the biggest one came at the end of our convention. We needed two-thirds of the states to **ratify**, or approve, the new Constitution, but the delegates were divided. Some supported the Constitution as we had written it, while others insisted it would give too much control to the U.S. government, and it did not include a list of basic rights and freedoms for individuals. Turns out, they had an idea about how to address these problems and change the Constitution.

I'm afraid this constitution gives too much power to the U.S. government. We need a list of rights to protect the people.

No we don't. The three branches of government have separate powers, and these branches will protect the rights of the people. Anyway, there are too many individual rights to list them all separately.

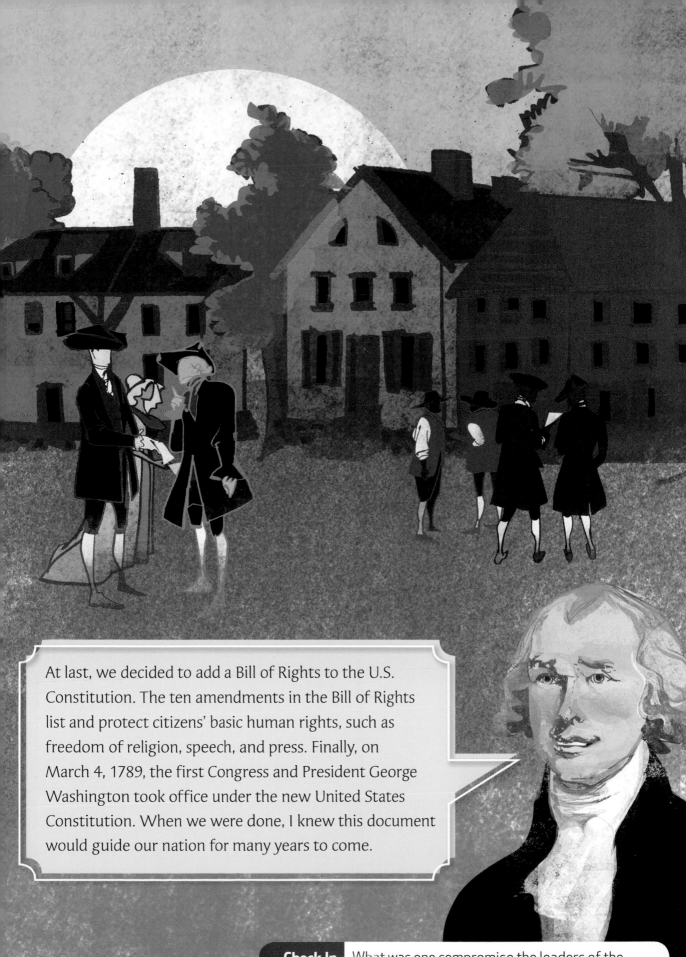

At last, we decided to add a Bill of Rights to the U.S. Constitution. The ten amendments in the Bill of Rights list and protect citizens' basic human rights, such as freedom of religion, speech, and press. Finally, on March 4, 1789, the first Congress and President George Washington took office under the new United States Constitution. When we were done, I knew this document would guide our nation for many years to come.

Check In What was one compromise the leaders of the states made as they wrote the U.S. Constitution?

WE THE PEOPLE

by Becky Manfredini

In this painting, *Scene at the Signing of the Constitution of the United States* (1940), state representatives sign the new U.S. Constitution.

Great as it is, our Constitution isn't perfect. Fortunately, the Founders realized that as times change, our Constitution might need to change too. They made sure that the citizens of the United States could choose to amend the U.S. Constitution, but they didn't make it easy. All amendments must be passed by Congress and ratified, or approved, by two-thirds of the states. Since the Bill of Rights was added in 1791, only 17 more amendments have

been added, for a total of 27. These 17 amendments reflect some of the most important decisions and issues in U.S. history. So let's see why some of the amendments were made and what impact they had on the United States. But remember—we only have time to highlight a few.

13th, 14th

FREE AT LAST!

The Thirteenth, Fourteenth, and Fifteenth Amendments were passed in the 1800s, many years after the Constitution was written. They were added to meet the needs of some of those not originally included in "We the People." You may remember that those are the first three words of the Preamble to the Constitution. You may also recall that when the Founders were writing the Constitution, they could not solve the problem of slavery in the United States. All people were not considered equal citizens, were not allowed to vote, and did not have basic rights. While some states and many people fought for the end of slavery, it took a long, bloody war to remedy this situation.

The war was the Civil War, and it began in 1861. This war between the states started in part because of a clash over slavery. People in the Southern states claimed they needed enslaved people to help work their farms. People in the Northern states did not allow slavery. Conflict over the issue led the South to break away from the United States, form its own country, and go to war with the rest of the United States.

After a long battle, the North won the war in 1865, and the country was reunited. Within five years, three important amendments became law. First, President Abraham Lincoln signed the Thirteenth Amendment in 1865, which abolished, or ended, slavery. Then the Fourteenth Amendment granted citizenship to formerly enslaved people in 1868. In 1870, the Fifteenth Amendment gave African American men the right to vote. However, it would take almost another 100 years to grant all African Americans true **civil rights**, including the right to equal education, employment, and housing.

⌄ **These newly freed African Americans were among about four million people freed by the Thirteenth Amendment.**

5th *Amendment*

THE RISE AND FALL OF AN AMENDMENT

The Eighteenth Amendment was passed, only to be struck down later by the Twenty-First Amendment. Here's what happened. In 1919, our nation was divided over the sale of alcoholic beverages such as beer and whiskey. Religious groups and women's organizations blamed the use of alcohol for destroying families. They demanded prohibiting, or not allowing, the sale of alcoholic beverages. In response, the government passed the Eighteenth Amendment, which made the manufacturing, sale, and transportation of alcoholic beverages illegal. This ban was called **Prohibition**.

But Prohibition didn't solve the nation's problems. In fact, it caused new ones. Many restaurants went out of business because they couldn't sell alcohol.

⌄ This is a typical Prohibition scene. Here, police are emptying barrels of beer and other alcoholic beverages into the public sewer.

18th Amendment

Because of Prohibition, thousands of people lost their jobs as servers, truckers, and factory workers. States that relied on the taxes from liquor sales couldn't pay their bills. But the growth of organized crime was probably the worst result of Prohibition.

Criminals seized the opportunity to form huge gangs across the country to supply people with illegal alcoholic beverages. Gangsters such as Al Capone made a lot of money selling illegal alcoholic beverages in the late 1920s and early 1930s, and crime and violence rose as rival gangs fought for territory to sell their illegal beverages. Instead of making people safer, the ban on alcohol made matters much worse. As a result, the government gave up on Prohibition. In 1933, Congress passed the Twenty-First Amendment to **repeal**, or end, Prohibition. As a result, the Eighteenth Amendment is the only amendment ever to be repealed.

∨ **This woman is expressing her support for an end to Prohibition.**

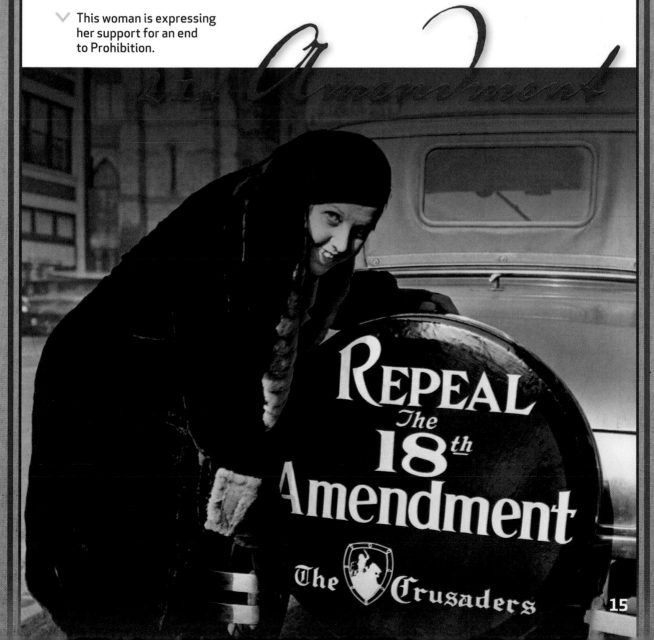

VOTES FOR ALL CITIZENS!

The Nineteenth, Twenty-Fourth, and Twenty-Sixth Amendments brought voting rights to new groups. Like African Americans, women had to wait until an amendment gave them **suffrage**, or the right to vote. For years, women marched and spoke out for their rights. Many were arrested and imprisoned for their actions. Finally in 1920, the Nineteenth Amendment was passed, and women in the United States gained the right to vote. After its passage, the nation had 26 million new voters—half the U.S. population at that time.

Another struggle for voting rights ended in 1964. Before this, African Americans in many states had to either take a test before they could vote or pay a "poll tax," which is a charge for voting. This often made voting more difficult even though it was their constitutional right.

∨ People who supported women's voting rights were called suffragists. These suffragists are marching in New York City in 1917.

In January 1964, Congress passed the Twenty-Fourth Amendment, making these unfair practices illegal.

Only one more group remained dissatisfied with their voting rights: 18-year-olds—and specifically 18-year-old men. In the 1960s and 1970s, the United States fought a war in Vietnam, in Southeast Asia. Any 18-year-old American man could be drafted for military service, and thousands fought and died in Vietnam.

Yet, according to the U.S. Constitution, no one under the age of 21 could vote.

Many people protested, pointing out that if 18-year-olds were old enough to fight in a war for their country, they should also be allowed to vote. As a result, the Twenty-Sixth Amendment passed in 1971, lowering the voting age for all American citizens to 18.

∨ A county clerk instructs an 18-year-old in how to use a voting machine so she can exercise her right to vote.

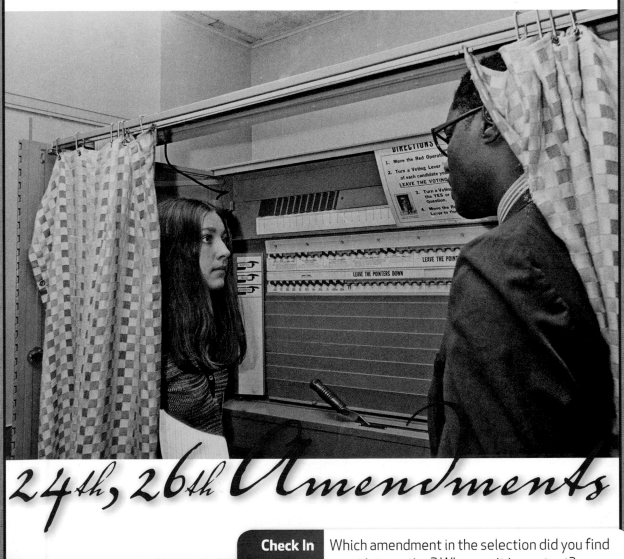

24th, 26th Amendments

Check In Which amendment in the selection did you find most interesting? Why was it important?

Failure Is Impossible

by Rosemary H. Knower

My wife's joined the Suffrage Movement,
(I've suffered ever since!)

Many cartoons of the 1800s and early 1900s made fun of suffragists, or people who fought for women's right to vote.

On August 26, 1995, the play "Failure Is Impossible" was read on the steps of the National Archives building in Washington, D.C. It was read to celebrate the 75th anniversary of the passage of the Nineteenth Amendment. The play tells the history of women's fight for voting rights in the United States.

Cast of Characters:

Narrator   Reader 1   Reader 2   Reader 3

Narrator: Today is the 75th anniversary of the passage of the Nineteenth Amendment, which gave women the right to vote. Did I hear you say, wait a minute—the country is 219 years old, and women have only been voting for 75 years? What's the problem here? It began with the words of the Founding Fathers: not the ones they put in, but the one they left out—"women." In 1776, when John Adams sat with a committee of men in Philadelphia, writing the Declaration of Independence, his wife Abigail wrote him:

Reader 1: John, in the new code of laws . . . remember the ladies. . . . Do not put such unlimited power in the hands of the husbands. Remember all men would be tyrants if they could. . . . We . . . will not hold ourselves bound by any laws in which we have no voice, or representation.

Narrator: But when the Founding Fathers wrote the Declaration and the Constitution, they stated: "We hold these truths to be self-evident, that all *men* are created equal." As a result, as of 1776, women could not vote or own property, and they had very few rights.

Songs and sayings helped motivate women during their fight for the right to vote. This is the cover for sheet music that was published in 1916.

Narrator: In 1848, a group of women organized the first Women's Rights Convention in Seneca Falls, New York. It took great courage. In the 1840s, respectable women did not even speak in public, let alone call meetings. Convention leader Elizabeth Cady Stanton said later:

Reader 1: We felt as helpless and hopeless as if we had suddenly been asked to construct a steam engine.

Narrator: But they were determined. They rewrote the Declaration of Independence to read: "We hold these truths to be self-evident: that all *men and women* are created equal." If women had the right to vote, they could defend themselves against men who took their wages or hurt them or their children. They needed more rights.

"Marching to Victory," was a song dedicated to suffragists around the world.

By 1900, over three million women worked for wages outside the home, often in hazardous and **exploitive** conditions, often with their children beside them at the machinery. They needed the ballot to give them a voice in making labor laws.

In the Triangle Shirtwaist Factory fire in 1911, 129 women were killed trying to escape an unsafe building into which they had been locked to keep them at work. Working women rushed to join the suffragist cause. With this new army of supporters, women succeeded in getting states to have **referendums**, or votes on one single issue—the issue of women's suffrage.

Reader 1: In 1912, the suffrage referendum was passed in Arizona, Kansas, and Oregon.

Reader 2: But defeated in Michigan, Ohio, and Wisconsin.

Narrator: In 1913, 5,000 women marched down Pennsylvania Avenue, in Washington, D.C., on the day before President Woodrow Wilson's inauguration, asking for the right to vote. They were mobbed by an angry crowd.

Reader 1: In 1914, the suffrage referendum passed in Montana and Nevada.

Reader 2: Defeated in North and South Dakota, Nebraska, and Missouri.

Reader 3: 1915: The suffrage referendum failed in New York, New Jersey, Pennsylvania, and Massachusetts.

Narrator: When the United States entered World War I in 1917, the government urged women to put aside their cause to help the war effort, just as the government had at the beginning of the Civil War in 1860. But in 1917, women worked for the war, and they also continued to work for the vote.

Reader 3 (reading from an eyewitness article)**:** In New York, more than a million women signed a **petition** asking for the right to vote. The petitions were pasted on signs carried by women marchers. The procession of the petitions alone covered more than half a mile.

Narrator: That same year, in Washington, D.C., other suffragists picketed outside the White House in rain and cold.

Reader 2: (Suffragist): Day after day, an intense silence would fall as the picketers were arrested. The watchers . . . saw not only younger women, but white-haired grandmothers, hoisted into the crowded patrol [wagon], their heads erect, and their frail hands holding tightly to the banner until [it was] wrested from them by brute force.

This was the cover of the official program of the women's suffrage march in 1913. Some onlookers made fun of the marchers.

This stamp and booklet urged Americans to give women the right to vote. The movement asked Americans to support women's suffrage with their votes.

We are ready
to Work beside You, Fight
beside You and Die beside You

Let Us Vote beside You

VOTE FOR

Candidates for the legislature
who stand for

Women
Working
in
Munition
Factory

**WOMAN
SUFFRAGE**

∧ Posters like this one asked voters to support candidates who would work for women's suffrage.

American Women

are urged to work in

Munition Plants
Railway Yards
Land Armies
Elevators
Trolley Cars
Ambulance Driving
Red Cross
Nursing, Etc.

**BUT in most
States They
are NOT
trusted
To Vote**

Enemy Aliens

are NOT trusted to work in

Munition Plants
Nor in many other war activities

BUT They ARE TRUSTED To Vote

In Eight States Foreigners Vote on First Papers.
In Nebraska in one County alone 785 men Claimed
Exemption from the Draft because they were
"Enemy Aliens," But Admitted They Had Voted
for years.

FOR THE HOME DEFENSE

Support those Candidates for the Legislature Who Stand for Woman Suffrage

∧ During World War I, women worked in many jobs important to the nation's defense.
But they could not vote.

Narrator: The White House pickets kept public attention focused on the issue. In 1917, at the height of World War I, President Wilson spoke to urge the Congress to act on suffrage.

Reader 3 (President Woodrow Wilson)**:** This is a people's war. Women think that democracy means that they should play their part alongside men and upon an equal footing with them.

Narrator: In January of 1918, the Nineteenth Amendment to give women the right to vote came before the House. However, it would be another year before the Senate passed the suffrage amendment, and another year beyond that before the necessary 36 states would ratify it.

Finally, on August 26, 1920, the Nineteenth Amendment gave women across the United States the right to vote. At the last Suffrage Convention of 1920, suffragist Carrie Chapman Catt spoke to the joyful women:

Reader 2: Ours has been a movement with a soul. Women came, served, and passed on, but others came to take their places. Who shall say that all the hosts of the millions of women who have toiled and hoped and met delay are not here today, and joining in the rejoicing? Their cause has won.

Check In What strategies did women use to win the vote?

Rosa Parks Says No

by Brinda Gupta

On the evening of December 1, 1955, a black woman named Rosa Parks took a seat on her usual bus in Montgomery, Alabama. As the bus filled with people, a white man approached Parks and motioned for her to get up. He wanted her seat. "No, I will not," Parks refused with calm dignity.

In 1955, people of different races weren't treated equally in the United States. In the South, **segregation**, or forced separation among races, was part of states' laws. Everyone could ride the bus in Montgomery, but black passengers had to sit in the back. And if the seats in the front filled up, white passengers could force black passengers to give up those seats to them. Black passengers who refused to do so were considered to be breaking local segregation laws.

Rosa Parks had been fighting for African American civil rights for years, but she had never before broken the law. "When I made that decision," Parks said later, "I knew that I had the strength of my ancestors with me." Her brave act was an example of **civil disobedience**, or a nonviolent form of protest against a law or policy.

Her simple refusal set a chain of events in motion that changed U.S. history. Her actions helped to spark the Civil Rights Movement, a struggle to win equal rights for African Americans. The Civil Rights Movement finally brought African Americans the rights guaranteed them in the Fourteenth Amendment—the rights of full citizenship. The movement also helped African Americans exercise the right to vote promised by the Fifteenth Amendment.

> Rosa Parks poses for a photo on a bus much like the one she had boarded when she refused to give up her seat.

"I know someone had to take the first step, and I made up my mind not to move. Our mistreatment was just not right, and I was tired of it." —ROSA PARKS

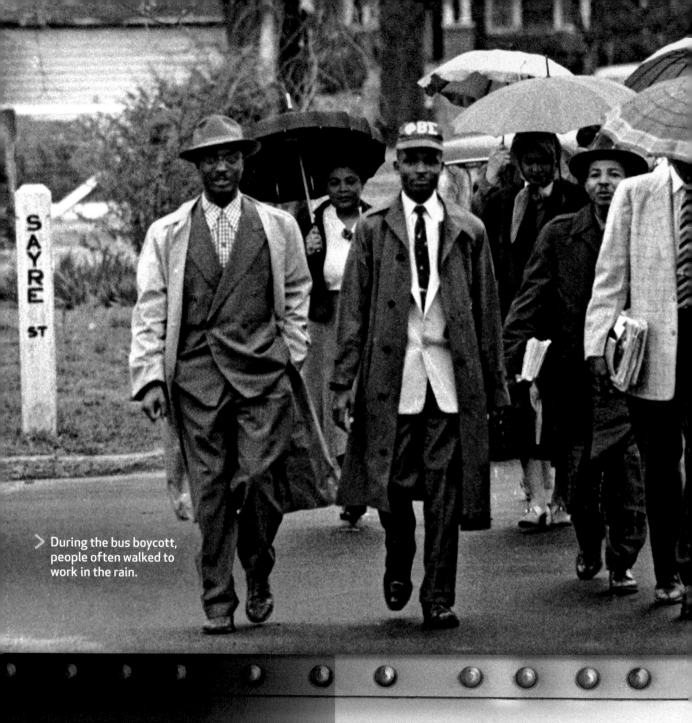

> During the bus boycott, people often walked to work in the rain.

Boycott!

When people in the African American community in Montgomery heard Parks's story, they knew they had to support her. They too were fed up with segregation. Civil rights groups met to discuss what action they would take, and they decided to stage a **boycott** of the Montgomery

buses until the unfair laws were changed. During a boycott, people refuse to buy a good or service in order to make a point. In Montgomery, many African Americans rode city buses. In fact, they made up about 75 percent of the total passengers, and the bus fares they paid helped to run the city. What better way of sending a

Few people rode the buses in Montgomery during the boycott. As a result, the bus companies lost more and more money.

message to the bus companies and the city than to stop using the bus system that treated them so unfairly?

It took many people and a lot of planning to make the boycott happen. People with cars gave rides to former bus riders. And many people simply walked instead of riding the bus. Even in bad weather and over long distances, people walked to work, school, and church, and to run errands. The first day of the boycott was a great success. Lines of walkers snaked through the city past empty buses. But that first day was only the beginning. Leaders encouraged people to keep it up, and the Montgomery bus boycott lasted a staggering 381 days.

The boycott was hurting the city of Montgomery and the bus companies financially, but the city and the state were reluctant to let go of the segregation laws. Finally, lawyers took the case to the U.S. Supreme Court, arguing that segregation laws went against the Constitution. The Court agreed. On November 13, 1956, it ruled that Montgomery's buses could no longer be segregated. About a month later, African Americans returned to riding the buses—and they could finally sit where they pleased.

The Montgomery bus boycott was one of the most successful protests against racial segregation in history. Nobody resorted to violence. No property was damaged. People simply chose not to support an unjust system.

As for Parks, she spent the rest of her life working for civil rights. She received many honors for her role and has been called the "Mother of the Civil Rights Movement." Perhaps most importantly, Parks inspired others by setting a good example. People who considered themselves ordinary citizens saw that Parks had made an enormous difference just by being brave enough to stand up for her beliefs.

This nine-foot-tall statue in Washington, D.C., honors Rosa Parks.

President Barack Obama visits the bus that Rosa Parks made famous. Today, the bus is on exhibit at the Henry Ford Museum in Michigan.

"...a single mo... ...mplest of... ...change America and chang... the world." —BARACK OBAMA

Check In How did one action by Rosa Parks help change our country?

Discuss

1. What connections can you make among the five selections in this book? How are the selections related?

2. Choose one amendment. How did the passing of that amendment show the country's ability to change with changing times?

3. Why do you think it took so long for American women to win the right to vote? How do you think women voters have changed the United States?

4. How can civil disobedience change unjust laws or government policies? Support your answer with details from the text.

5. What do you still wonder about the U.S. Constitution? How can you find out more?